Oranges and Lemons

Compiled by Karen King   Illustrated by Ian Beck

OXFORD
UNIVERSITY PRESS

Contents

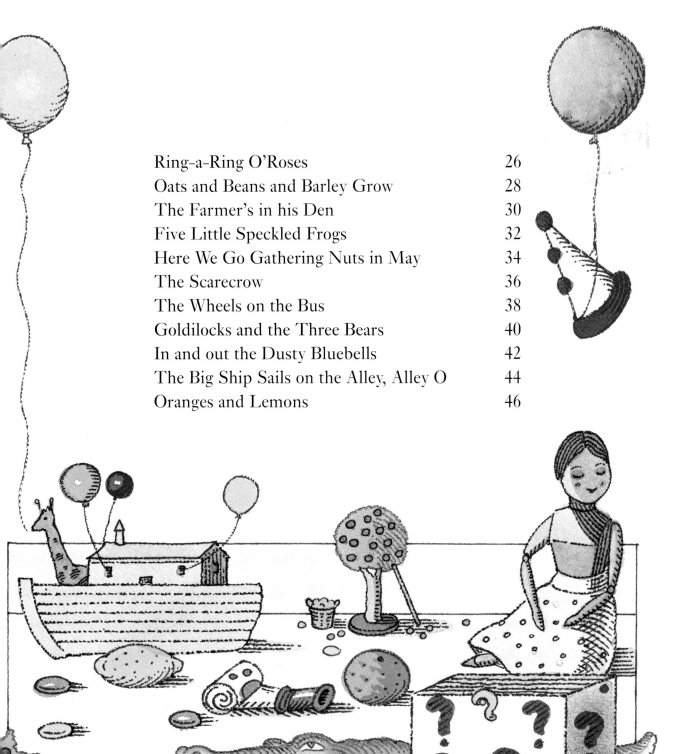

This action song for younger children is easy to learn and it has the same tune as 'Here we go round the Mulberry Bush'. Play it two or three times as toddlers especially love popping up and down like a real Jack-in-the-Box.

Everyone crouch down as low as possible. Pretend you are a Jack-in-the-Box, coiled up inside, waiting for someone to come along and press the button to open the lid.

Pretend to press a 'release button' on top of head and leap to feet with arms outstretched. Bob up and down as if on a spring and then waggle head.

Put both hands on top of head and push yourself down into a crouching position, as if the Jack-in-the-Box is being pushed back into his box.

1

2

3

Jack-in-the-Box...

...Jumps up like this!
He makes me laugh as he waggles his head...

I gently press him down again
Saying: 'Jack-in-the-Box
You must go to bed.'

Jack- in- the- box — jumps up like this! He makes me laugh as he wag - gles his head. I

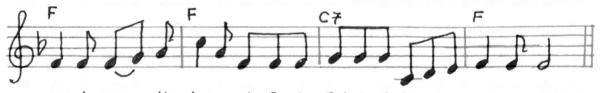

gent - ly press — him down a - gain, Say - ing 'Jack- in- the box, you must go to bed.'

6

Jack-in-the-box

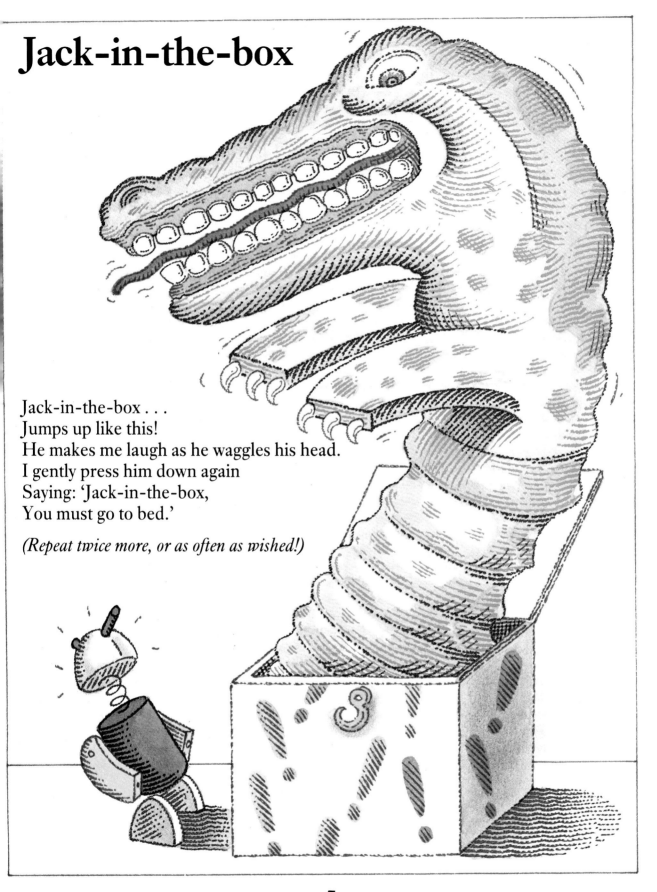

Jack-in-the-box . . .
Jumps up like this!
He makes me laugh as he waggles his head.
I gently press him down again
Saying: 'Jack-in-the-box,
You must go to bed.'

(Repeat twice more, or as often as wished!)

This song has the same tune as 'Ten Green Bottles', and is just right for younger children to learn, although the older ones may find it rather boring. You can alter the number of children as required, though remember that any number over five can be a little difficult for the three and four year olds to cope with.

Age: 2–4
Number of children:
Five

Choose five children and place them, sitting in a row. Everybody sings together. On the first verse, one child gently falls backwards, and lies there until the end of the song. On the second verse, the next child does the same, and so on, until they are all lying down.

Five brown ted - dies sit - ting on a wall. Five brown ted - dies

sit - ting on a wall, And if one brown ted - dy should

ac - ci - dent - ally fall, There'd be four brown ted - dies sit - ting on a wall.

(Guitarists may prefer to capo up 3 frets and play in key of D. Use chords D, A7 and G.)

Five Brown Teddies

1. Five brown teddies sitting on a wall.
   Five brown teddies sitting on a wall.
   And if one brown teddy should accidentally fall
   There'd be four brown teddies sitting on a wall.

2. Four brown teddies sitting on a wall, etc.
3. Three brown teddies sitting on a wall, etc.
4. Two brown teddies sitting on a wall, etc.
5. One brown teddy sitting on a wall.
6. And if one brown teddy should accidentally fall,
   There'd be no brown teddies sitting there at all!

A good group song which children particularly enjoy as they can suggest their own verses and the tune is very easy to learn. Remember to start circling again when singing the chorus after each verse.

Age: 3+
Number of children:
four or more

Form a ring, join hands and walk or skip round singing the chorus.
1

Stop circling and pretend to wash face.
2

This is the way we wash our face . . .

Stop circling and pretend to brush hair.
3

. . . brush our hair . . .

'Here we go round the mulberry bush . . .'

Stop circling and pretend to brush teeth.
4

. . . clean our teeth . . .

Stop circling and pretend to put clothes on – jumper, trousers, socks, etc.
5

. . . put on our clothes . . .

Here we go round the mul - berry bush, the mul - berry bush, the mul - berry bush,

Here we go round the mul - berry bush, On a cold and fro - sty morn - ing.

Here we go round the mulberry bush

Chorus:
Here we go round the mulberry bush,
The mulberry bush, the mulberry bush,
Here we go round the mulberry bush,
On a cold and frosty morning.

1. This is the way we wash our hands,
Wash our hands, wash our hands,
This is the way we wash our hands,
On a cold and frosty morning.

2. This is the way we wash our face, etc.

3. This is the way we brush our hair, etc.

4. This is the way we clean our teeth, etc.

5. This is the way we put on our clothes, etc.

(Remember to sing the chorus after each verse.)

A noisy, lively song, for which you can invent your own verses with other pretend instruments. Real instruments can be used to great effect – shakers, elastic bands stretched over boxes, two sticks clapped together, coconut shells, margarine tubs filled with rice, etc. (although some ingenuity is needed to invent names for things that fit in with the three-syllable rhythm e.g. big-bass-drum.)

Age: 2½+
Number of children:
Any

Pretend to hold a drumstick in each hand and 'pound' the drum.
2

... on the big bass drum ...

Play on an imaginary violin with a 'bow'.
3

... on the violin ...

Form a semi-circle in front of the conductor (a grown-up or leader of the game).
1

'Oh we can play ...'

Pretend to dangle a triangle in one hand, and 'hit' it with the index finger of the other hand.
4

... on the triangle ...

Put both hands to one side of face, palms facing inwards, and wiggle fingers, as if playing flute.
5

... on the silver flute ...

Oh, — we can play on the big bass drum And this is the way we do it, Boom, boom, boom, goes the big bass drum And that's the way we do it.

Oh, we can play on the big bass drum

Oh, we can play on the big bass drum
And this is the way we do it,
BOOM, BOOM, BOOM, goes the big bass drum
And that's the way we do it.

Oh, we can play on the violin, etc.
(FIDDLE-DIDDLE-DEE)

Oh, we can play on the triangle, etc.
(TING, TING, TING)

Oh, we can play on the silver flute, etc.
(TOOTLE-OOTLE-OOT)

13

This is a lovely 'story' song which is not too difficult to learn. Dressing up clothes are a good idea though not a necessity. (*Princess* – a pretty dress, cardboard crown; *Wicked Fairy* – black paper cone for witch's hat, cape, stick for wand: *Handsome Prince* – broom for horse, cloak, wellington boots, wooden sword).

Age: 3½+
Number of Children:
  Six or more

1. Everybody makes a ring. A girl is chosen to be Princess and she stands in the middle of the ring.

2. Everybody except the Princess raise their joined hands to make a tower.

3. A child is chosen to be fairy and she comes out of the ring and waves her wand over the Princess. Everybody else waves their index fingers.

4. The Princess lies down and pretends to be asleep. All the other children lay their heads on hands and close their eyes.

There was a Princess long ago...

And she dwelt in a big, high tower...

A wicked fairy cast a spell...

The Princess slept for a hundred years...

5. Everybody in the ring stands closer, and intertwines arms in an upward movement as if they are trees growing.

6. A boy is chosen to be prince and he gallops round the outside of the ring. The Prince pretends to strike each 'tree' with a sword. As the Prince touches him each child then falls down like a tree that has been felled.

7. The Prince enters the ring of fallen 'trees' and kisses the Princess. Children are sometime loath to do this! In this case quickly substitute 'He took her hand to wake her up...

8. Everyone now jumps up and claps hands in time to the tune.

A great big forest grew around...

A handsome Prince came riding by...
He chopped the trees down...

He woke the Princess with a kiss.

So everybody's happy now...

1. There was a prin-cess long a - go, long a - go,

long a - go, There was a prin-cess long a - go, long, long a - go.

Sleeping Beauty

1. There was a princess long ago, long ago, long ago,
   There was a princess long ago, long, long ago.

2. And she dwelt in a big, high tower, a big, high tower, a big, high tower,
   And she dwelt in a big, high tower, long, long ago.

3. A wicked fairy cast a spell, etc.

4. The princess slept for a hundred years, etc.

5. A great big forest grew around, etc.

6. A handsome prince came riding by, etc.

7. He chopped the trees down one by one, etc.

8. He woke the princess with a kiss, etc.

9. So everybody's happy now, happy now, happy now,
   So everybody's happy now, happy now!

This song is very good for counting practice, and introduces children to the lovely old Bible story. If you are singing this with a group of children, choose beforehand the child who is to slam a door on the last verse. If you have heavy doors, or glass doors, it is much safer to have an imaginary one!

Hold up eight fingers, then look and point to wristwatch, (real or imaginary).

5

Now in came the animals eight
by eight,
some were on time and some
were late...

Hold two fingers up on one hand.

2

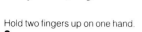

Now in came the animals
two by two...

Everyone sings the chorus while putting one fist on top of the other to 'build' the ark. The chorus is sung and the ark built after each verse.

1

Who built the Ark? Noah! Noah!...

Hold up four fingers, then point to a window and a door with the other hand.

3

Hold up six fingers, then laugh soundlessly while tickling yourself under one arm like a monkey.

4

Hold up ten fingers, then put them down. Hold up five for the roosters, then five for the hens.

6

Now in came the animals four
by four,
two through the window and two
through the door...

Now in came the animals six by six, the elephants
laughed at the monkeys' tricks...

Now in came the animals ten
by ten,
five black roosters and five
black hens...

Who built the Ark? No - ah! No - ah! Who built the Ark? Bro - ther

No - ah built the Ark. 1. Now in came the an - i - mals two, by two The

hip - po - pot - a - mus and the kan - ga - roo.

Noah's Ark

Chorus:
Who built the Ark?
Noah! Noah!
Who built the Ark?
Brother Noah built the Ark.

1. Now in came the animals two by two,
   The hippopotamus and the kangaroo.

2. Now in came the animals four by four,
   Two through the window and two through the door.

3. Now in came the animals six by six,
   The elephants laughed at the monkey's tricks.

4. Now in came the animals eight by eight,
   Some were on time and some were late.

5. Now in came the animals ten by ten,
   Five black roosters and five black hens.

6. Now Noah said: 'Go and SHUT THAT DOOR!
   The rain's started falling and we can't take more.'

(Remember to sing the Chorus after each verse)

This is a lively song with a tune that is easy to remember. Adults tend to be more worried about the words than children, who think the scarier the better!

Everyone raise arms above the head and sway from left to right.
2

They planted an apple tree over his head...

Everybody forms a ring. One child is chosen to be 'Old Roger'. 'Old Roger' lies down in the centre of the ring.
1

Old Roger is dead and he lies in his grave...

Choose a child to be the 'Old Woman'. The Old Woman pretends to pick up apples and put them in her apron.
4

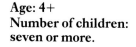

There came an old woman a-picking them up...

'Roger' gets up and *gently* pokes the 'Old Woman'.
5

Everyone makes fists for 'Apples' and then drops their hands and waggles their fingers to show them 'tumbling down'.
3

The apples grew ripe and they all tumbled down...

Old Roger got up and he gave her a poke...

1. Old Ro - ger is dead and he lies in his grave, Lies in his grave,

lies in his grave. Old Ro - ger is dead and he lies in his grave,

Heigh - ho, lies in his grave.

Old Roger is dead

1. Old Roger is dead and he lies in his grave,
   Lies in his grave, lies in his grave.
   Old Roger is dead and he lies in his grave,
   Heigh ho, lies in his grave.

2. They planted an apple tree over his head, etc.
3. The apples grew ripe and they all tumbled down, etc.
4. There came an old woman a-picking them up, etc.
5. Old Roger got up and he gave her a poke, etc.

6. This made the old woman go hippety-hop,
   Hippety-hop, hippety-hop,
   This made the old woman go hippety-hop,
   Heigh-ho, hippety-hop.

This lovely dancing song is a good way of introducing the concept of left and right to young children. Don't worry, however, if the very young ones don't get it right; let them simply enjoy the actions of moving and shaking themselves about! Form a circle, join hands, and dance or skip around each time the chorus is sung. Perform the actions as described in the verses.

Everybody dances round during the chorus and does the appropriate actions during the verses.

Here we go Looby-Loo.

Chorus

Here we go loo - by loo, Here we go loo - by light,

Here we go loo - by loo, All on a Sat - ur - day night.

Verse

1. Put your right hand in, Put your right hand out, Shake it a lit - tle, a

lit - tle, And turn — your - self - a - bout.

20

Looby-loo

Chorus:
Here we go looby-loo
Here we go looby-light
Here we go looby-loo
All on a Saturday night.

1. Put your right hand in
   Put your right hand out
   Shake it a little, a little
   And turn yourself about.

2. Put your left hand in, etc.
3. Put your right foot in, etc.
4. Put your left foot in, etc.
5. Put your whole self in, etc.

(Don't forget to sing the Chorus after each verse)

If you are in a large room, you can march across to one side of the room for the top of the hill; back to the other side for the bottom; and in the middle for half-way up. This is noisy, and the song won't be sung smoothly, but it is more realistic, and children enjoy pretending to be soldiers marching along. Alternatively everyone can use their fingers to make all the marching actions.

Everybody sing together and march across
the room and back again.
1

All stand up. All sit down.
2

All crouch half-way between
standing and sitting.
3

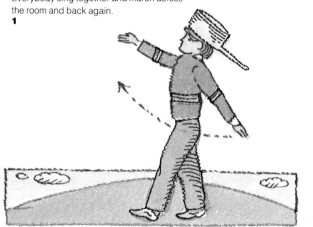

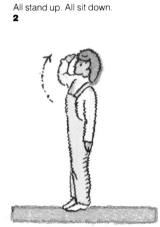

**And when they were down,
they were down**

Stand up again. Sit down again.
4

**He marched them up to the top of the hill and he marched them down
again . . .**

**And when they were up,
they were up**

**And when they were only
They were neither up nor down**

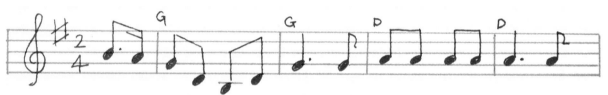

Oh, the grand old Duke of York, He had ten thou-sand men, He

marched them up to the top of the hill And he marched them down a - gain. And

when they were up they were up, And when they were down they were

down. And when they were on - ly half- way up They were nei -ther up nor down,

The grand old Duke of York

1. Oh, the grand old Duke of York,
He had ten thousand men.
He marched them up to the top of the hill
And he marched them down again.

Chorus:
And when they were up they were up,
And when they were down they were down,
And when they were only half-way up
They were neither up nor down.

2. Oh, the grand old Duke of York,
He had ten thousand men.
They beat their drums to the top of the hill
And they beat them down again.

3. They played their pipes to the top of the hill,

4. They banged their guns to the top of the hill,

This is so popular that it hardly needs an introduction. It can be played with the tiniest toddlers, who will probably be happy with the first verse over and over again! The extra verses add more interest for older children.

Age: 2+
Number of children:
Any

Make a ring, link hands and circle singing each verse together.
1

Ring a ring o'roses...

Bump down on to floor on the word 'down'.
2

... atishoo, atishoo, we all fall down.
5 Bump down again on the word 'down'. Stay down until last line of next verse.

Kneel down on the word 'kneel.'
3

... atishoo, atishoo, we all kneel down.

Turn on to all fours and pretend to be a cow chewing the cud. Leap up quickly on to feet and shout 'not me!'
6/7

... atishoo, atishoo, who's up last?...
... Not me!

Bow as if to the king, on the word 'bow'
4

... atishoo, atishoo, we all bow down.

Ring- a- ring o' ro- ses, A- pock- et full of po- sies, A-

tish - oo! A- tish - oo! We all fall down.

26

Ring-a-ring o'roses

Ring-a-ring o'roses,
A pocket full of posies,
A-tishoo! A-tishoo!
We all fall down.

The bird is on the steeple,
High above the people,
A-tishoo! A-tishoo!
We all kneel down.

The king has sent his daughter,
To fetch a pail of water,
A-tishoo! A-tishoo!
We all bow down.

The wedding bells are ringing,
The children they are singing,
A-tishoo! A-tishoo!
We all fall down.

The cows are in the meadow,
Eating all the grass,
A-tishoo! A-tishoo!
Who's up last?
NOT ME!

This is a lovely old fashioned dancing song; just right for harvest time, but can be used at any time of the year. A particular favourite with infant school children.

Age: 4+
Number of children:
four or more

Pretend to hold a basket under one arm, and scoop out the seed, scattering it towards the centre of the ring.
2

**First the farmer sows
his seed...**

Form a ring, link hands, walk or dance around and everybody sings the first verse.
1

Oats and beans and barley grow...

Stamp feet, then clap hands.
4

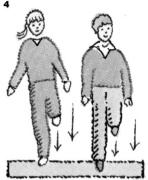

**He stamps his feet and claps
his hands...**

Stand with legs apart, and rest hands on hips.
3

**Then he stands and takes
his ease...**

Turn about, pretending to look all over the land.
5

**Then turns him round to
view the land.**

1. Oats and beans and bar-ley grow, Oats and beans and bar-ley grow, But not

you nor I nor an-y-one know How oats and beans and bar-ley grow.

Oats and Beans and Barley Grow

1. Oats and beans and barley grow,
   Oats and beans and barley grow,
   But not you nor I nor anyone know,
   How oats and beans and barley grow.

2. First the farmer sows his seed,
   Then he stands and takes his ease,
   Stamps his feet and claps his hands
   And turns him round to view the land.

On the last verse I have used 'clap the bone', instead of the more traditional 'pat the bone'. If you prefer to use the latter, however, then the 'bone' is *gently* patted on the head. I emphasise 'gently', as the 'bone' can get hurt if everyone pats him too enthusiastically!

Age: 3+
Number of children:
ten or more

Choose a child to be a farmer. The farmer stands in the centre of a circling ring of children. Everybody sings.

1

The farmer's in his den...

The farmer chooses a child from the ring to be his wife. She joins him in the centre

2

The farmer wants a wife...

The child, nurse, dog and bone are selected in turn, and then everyone gathers around the bone, clapping hands in time to the tune.

3

We all clap the bone...

1. The far-mer's in his den, The far-mer's in his den.

Ee - aye - ee - aye, The far-mer's in his den.

30

The Farmer's in his den

1. The farmer's in his den
   The farmer's in his den
   Eee–Aye–Eee–Aye
   The farmer's in his den.

2. The farmer wants a wife, etc.

3. The wife wants a child, etc.

4. The child wants a nurse, etc.
5. The nurse wants a dog, etc.
6. The dog wants a bone, etc.
7. We all clap the bone, etc.

This is a action song game for younger children. If you have a large number of children, they can be divided into groups of five, one group being 'frogs' first, while the others sing and count. The number of frogs can be adapted to three, four, six, or any number you like. Remember not to have too high a number with young children.

Age: 3+
Number of children:
    Any

One child leaps into the centre of the ring, and remains there until end of song. On each verse, thereafter, one more child leaps into the 'pool', until no more are left in the ring.

Choose five children and place then, squatting, in a well-spaced ring Everybody sings the song together.

Each child pretends to eat with one hand and rub tummy with the other.

1

Five little speckled frogs, sat on a speckled log...

2

... Eating some most delicious bugs, yum! yum!

3

One jumped into the pool...

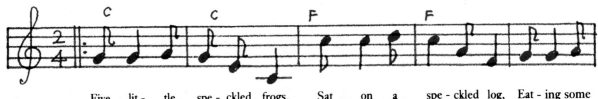

Five lit - tle spe - ckled frogs,   Sat on a   spe - ckled log, Eat - ing some
One jumped in - to   the   pool, Where it was   nice and cool, Now there are

most de - li - cious   bugs, Yum! Yum!
four more   spe - ckled

frogs, Glub!   Glub!

Five little speckled frogs

1. Five little speckled frogs
   Sat on a speckled log,
   Eating some most delicious bugs,
   Yum! Yum!
   One jumped into the pool,
   Where it was nice and cool,
   Now there are four more speckled
   frogs Glub! Glub!

2. Four little speckled frogs, etc.
3. Three little speckled frogs, etc.
4. Two little speckled frogs, etc.
5. One little speckled frog, etc. . . .

. . . Now there are no more speckled
frogs, Glub! Glub!

This is an old fashioned dancing song enjoyed particularly by older children who are able to skip rhythmically in time to the tune. It can be quite a lengthy game, so if you wish, a time limit can be set before starting, at the end of which the side with the most children are the winners.

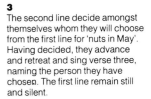

1
Divide everybody into two groups of roughly equal numbers. The groups form two lines, facing each other, holding hands. During the first verse both lines dance towards and away from each other.
Here we go gathering nuts in May...

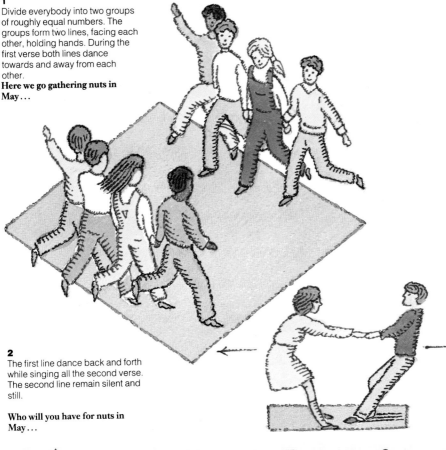

3
The second line decide amongst themselves whom they will choose from the first line for 'nuts in May'. Having decided, they advance and retreat and sing verse three, naming the person they have chosen. The first line remain still and silent.

We'll have 'Thomas' for nuts in May...

4
The first line dance and sing verse four. The second line choose, and dance and sing verse five.

Who will you send to fetch him away...

We'll send 'Helen' to fetch him away...

2
The first line dance back and forth while singing all the second verse. The second line remain silent and still.

Who will you have for nuts in May...

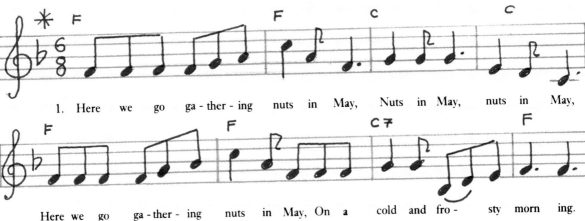

5
'Helen' and 'Thomas' now have a tug-of-war. The loser of the tug-of-war has to join the winner's side. The game is then repeated until one side has won all the children from the other side, or the game has been played for an agreed number of times.

1. Here we go ga-ther-ing nuts in May, Nuts in May, nuts in May,

Here we go ga-ther-ing nuts in May, On a cold and fro-sty morn ing.

Here we go gathering nuts in May

1. Here we go gathering nuts in May,
   Nuts in May, nuts in May,
   Here we go gathering nuts in May,
   On a cold and frosty morning.

2. Who will you have for nuts in May? etc.

3. We'll have 'Thomas' for nuts in May, etc.

4. Who will you send to fetch him away? etc.

5. We'll send 'Helen' to fetch him away, etc.

This is a well-known song amongst young children. It can be very noisy, particularly on the second verse, but it is a great ice-breaker, and good for using up surplus energy at parties.

Crouch or lie down on floor, eyes closed.

1

When all the cows were sleeping, and the sun had gone to bed...

Leap onto feet.

2

Up jumped the scarecrow, and this is what he said...

Stretch arms out sideways, hands dangling. With feet apart, rock stiffly from side to side, first standing on one leg, then on the other.

3

I'm a dingle-dangle scarecrow...

Nod head two or three times.

4

With a flippy, floppy hat...

Shake both arms vigorously, then shake legs – first one, then the other.

5

I can shake my arms like this, I can shake my legs like that.

Actions for the second verse are the same as for the first but sing very loudly when the scarecrow has jumped to his feet.

When all the cows — were sleep-ing, And the sun had gone — to bed,

Up jumped the scare-crow and this is what he said: 'I'm a

din-gle dan-gle scare-crow with a flip-py flop-py hat. I can

shake my arms like this, I can shake my legs like that.'

The Scarecrow

When all the cows were sleeping,
And the sun had gone to bed,
Up jumped the scarecrow,
And this is what he said:
'I'm a dingle-dangle scarecrow,
With a flippy-floppy hat,
I can shake my arms like this,
I can shake my legs like that.'

When all the hens were roosting,
And the moon behind a cloud,
Up jumped the scarecrow,
And shouted very loud:
'I'M A DINGLE-DANGLE SCARECROW,
WITH A FLIPPY-FLOPPY HAT!
I CAN SHAKE MY ARMS LIKE THIS,
I CAN SHAKE MY LEGS LIKE THAT!'

A good action song which requires little space. Once learned younger children refuse to get fed up with it. Remember to use the 'babies on the bus' *after* 'the children on the bus' if you want to quieten an over-enthusiastic lot down.

Everyone stand (or sit) and sing and perform actions together. Bend arms at elbow and keeping close to sides, hold hands straight out in front. Then rotate arms as if wheels.
1

The wheels on the bus...

Hold up hands in front of face palms facing outwards Sway hands from left to right for wipers.
2

The wipers on the bus...

Make a fist with hand and jab imaginary horn button with thumb.
3

The driver on the bus...

Pretend to gently guide a passenger along.

The conductor on the bus...

Open and shut hands rhythmically as if they are mouths chattering. Sing louder for 'Yakkity-Yak!'.
5

The mummies on the bus...

Put both hands over ears and screw up face as if you can't bear the noise. Shout at top of voice for 'Too Much Noise'.
6

The children on the bus...

Pretend to go to sleep. Sing this verse quietly.
7

The babies on the bus...

The wheels on the bus go round and round, Round and round, Round and round. The wheels on the bus go round and round, All day long.

The wheels on the bus

1. The wheels on the bus go round and round,
   Round and round, round and round.
   The wheels on the bus go round and round,
   All day long.

2. The wipers on the bus go swish, swish, swish, etc.
3. The driver on the bus goes 'Toot! Toot! Toot! etc.
4. The conductor on the bus says: 'Hurry along please!'
5. The mummies on the bus go 'Yakkity-yak!' etc.
6. The children on the bus make TOO MUCH NOISE!, etc.
7. The babies on the bus fall fast asleep, etc.

Children of all ages like to act out this old familiar tale and to sing the words. You could start off by telling the story and then finish by dancing and singing it.

Everybody point hands together to make 'roof' shape and begin to sing the song.
1

When Goldilocks went to the house of the bears...

Point index fingers to eyes.
2

Oh, what did her blue eyes see.

Use hands and arms to make bowl shapes, large, smaller, and lastly a very tiny one.
3

A bowl that was huge ... small ... tiny, and that was all ...

Point index finger to left ('one'), to middle ('two'), then to the right ('three').
4

And she counted them one, two, three ...

Raise one hand high above floor level for 'huge', lower for 'small', and just above ground for 'tiny'.
5

A chair that was huge ... small ... tiny, and that was all ...

Stretch arms out wide and bring hands together to follow words
6

A bed that was huge ... small ... tiny, and that was all ...

Raise both arms high above head, bring down to half-way down for 'small', knee level for 'tiny'
7

A bear that was huge ... small ... tiny, and that was all ...

Pretend to be fiercely growling bears. 'Claw' the air, first to the left (ROARR!); to the middle (ROARR!), and then to the right (ROARR!).
8

And they growled at her. ROARR! ROARR! ROARR!

Chorus

When Gold-i-locks went to the house of the bears, Oh, what did her

blue eyes see? — 1. A bowl that was huge, and a bowl that was

small, And a bowl that was ti-ny and that was all, And she count-ed them —

one, two, three.

40

Goldilocks and the three bears

Chorus:
When Goldilocks went to the house of the bears
Oh, what did her blue eyes see?

1. A bowl that was huge and a bowl that was small,
   And a bowl that was tiny and that was all,
   And she counted them – one, two, three.

2. A chair that was huge and a chair that was small, etc.

3. A bed that was huge and a bed that was small, etc.

4. A bear that was huge and a bear that was small,
   And a bear that was tiny and that was all,
   And they growled at her – ROARR! ROARR! ROARR!

A delightful, old dancing game, which has a kind of 'follow-my-leader' theme. It is a popular one in the playground with infant school children, although it is equally good at parties.

Age: 4+
Number of children:
ten or more.

Choose a child to be the leader. The rest of the children form a ring, with hands joined, and raise their arms to form arches. The leader then weaves in and out of the arches.

1

In and out the dusty bluebells...

At the end of the first verse, the leader goes to stand behind one of the children in the ring and taps his shoulders with alternate hands, rhythmically.

2

Tippy-tappy tap-toe on my shoulder...

The child whose shoulders have been tapped becomes the leader. The ring closes and the first child holds on to the new leader's waist as they both weave in and out of the arches.

3

4

The song is repeated, the weaving line grows longer and the ring smaller until the ring becomes too small to weave in and out of. Whereupon the game is over and everybody falls in a heap!

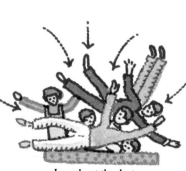

In and out the dusty bluebells...

In and out the dust-y blue-bells, In and out the

dust-y blue-bells, In and out the dust-y blue-bells, Who will be my mas-ter?

Tip-py-tip-py tap-toe on my shoul-der, Tip-py-tip-py tap-toe on my shoul-der,

Tip-py-tip-py tap-toe on my shoul-der, You will be my mas-ter.

42

In and out the dusty bluebells

In and out the dusty bluebells,
In and out the dusty bluebells,
Who will be my master?

Tippy-tippy tap-toe on my shoulder,
Tippy-tippy tap-toe on my shoulder,
Tippy-tippy tap-toe on my shoulder,
You will be my master.

This is a traditional, and very popular action song for older children. It is ingenious and intricate, hard to describe but fun to play.

Age: 6+

Number of children: Any

The children form a long line, holding hands. One of the end children rests his hand against a wall to form an arch. The child at the other end leads the line under the arch, and everybody starts to sing.

1

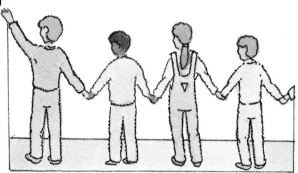

The big ship sails on the Alley, Alley O...

As the last child goes through the arch, he twists the first child's arms so that they are crossed against the wall. The last child now stands next to the first child, and puts his hands on the wall, to form another arch.

2

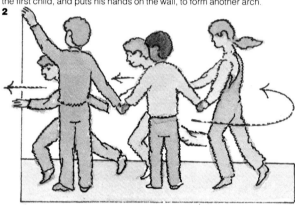

... On the last day of September...

There are now two arches. The line of children come back under them, and the last child to go through forms another arch, and so on. The first verse is repeated until all the children have crossed arms.

3

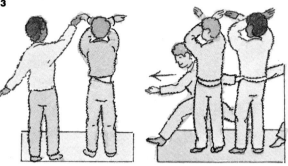

The big ship sails on the Alley, Alley O ... on the last day of September.

The children now form a ring, holding hands with arms still crossed. For verse two everybody shakes their head gravely. For verse three, the ring squats down and rises up again keeping arms crossed. For verse four, everybody bends their heads as low as possible.

4

The Captain said: 'It will never, never do'...
The big ship sank to the bottom of the sea...
We all dip our heads in the deep, blue sea...

The big ship sails on the al - ley al - ley, O — the al - ley, al - ley O — the al - ley al - ley, O. Oh, the big ship sails on the al - ley, al - ley O, on the last day of Sep - tem - ber.—

The big ship sails on the alley, alley O

1. The big ship sails on the alley, alley O,
   The alley, alley O, the alley, alley O.
   The big ship sails on the alley, alley O,
   On the last day of September.

2. The captain said: 'It will never, never do, etc.

3. The big ship sank to the bottom of the sea, etc.

4. We all dip our heads in the deep, blue sea,
   The deep, blue sea, the deep, blue sea,
   We all dip our heads in the deep, blue sea,
   On the last day of September.

Most people know this delightful game but have forgotten either the words or how to play it. Apart from the ringing melody the best bit for the players is as the suspense builds to the chanting of the final Chip! Chop! It can take quite a long time to play and so is excellent if you want to spin things out owing to an 'emergency' elsewhere. On the other hand if you want to shorten it then get the archway to capture more than one child at a time (see box 5).

Age: 3½+
Number of Children: eight or more

Choose the two tallest children and ask them to make an archway with their arms. (If the children aren't tall enough then find two 'willing' grown-ups.) Tell one to be 'oranges' and the other to be 'lemons'.

1

The other children form a line ready to go under the 'arch'. Then everybody starts to sing the song and the line of children begin to pass underneath the 'arch'.

2

Oranges and Lemons,
Say the bells of St Clements...

Everybody continues to sing the song and the children skip round to pass under the 'arch' again.

3

I owe you five farthings...
... says the great bell at Bow.

The last three lines (from 'Here comes the candle...) are chanted and the pace gets faster. On the last line the 'arch' pretends to chop each of the children as they pass underneath, one child for each 'chip' or 'chop'.

4

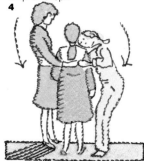

Chip, chop, chip, chop...

When they reach the words 'the last man's...HEAD! the arch brings down their arms together and encircles and captures a child (or more than one child if you want to speed things up and they are little enough!).

5

... the last man's ... HEAD!

The archway people now ask their captive to choose to be 'Oranges or Lemons?' (This must be whispered so that the others don't know which is which). Those who choose Oranges stand behind the Orange arch person and vice versa.

6

'Oranges or Lemons?'

The song is repeated continually until all the children have been captured and are standing behind either 'Orange' or 'Lemon'. They now face each other in two long lines, grasp each other around the waist and have a tug of war. The side which manages to pull the other across are then declared the winners!

7

Oran-ges and le-mons, Say the bells of Saint Cle-ments. I

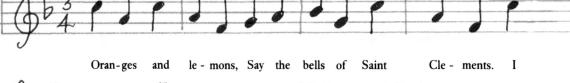

owe you five far-things, say the bells of Saint Mar-tins. When will you

Music continues over.

Oranges and Lemons

Oranges and lemons,
Say the bells of St. Clements,

I owe you five farthings,
Say the bells of St. Martins,

When will you pay me?
Say the bells of Old Bailey,

When I grow rich,
say the bells at Shoreditch,

When will that be?
Say the bells of Stepney,

I'm sure I don't know,
Says the great bell at Bow.

Here–comes–the–candle–to–light–you–to–bed,
Here–comes–the–chopper–to–chop–off–your–head,
Chip–chop–chip–chop–the–last–man's . . . HEAD

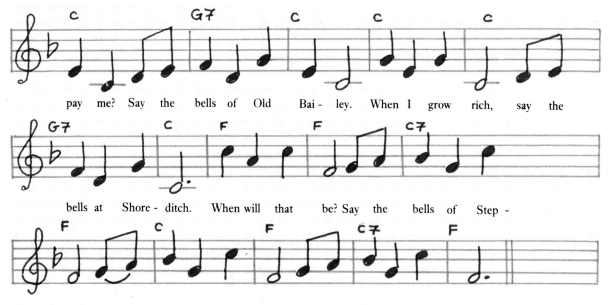

pay me? Say the bells of Old Bai - ley. When I grow rich, say the

bells at Shore - ditch. When will that be? Say the bells of Step -

ney. I'm — sure I don't know, says the great bell at Bow.